Old Friend
From Far Away

150 Chinese Poems from the Great Dynasties

Translated by
C. H. Kwock and Vincent McHugh

North Point Press
San Francisco
1980

有朋自遠方來不亦樂乎
　　　　　　　　　　— 論語

To have an old friend come from far away —
　　　　isn't it a joy!

The Analects

Acknowledgments

Our more-than-thanks to those scholar-friends who have taken time to help us with advice in all the knotty business of old Chinese poetry and old Mandarin.

We are grateful to, among others, the late Dr. Hu Shih, president of Academia Sinica, Taiwan; the late Chen Shih-hsiang, professor of Chinese literature at the University of California in Berkeley; Donald Keene of Columbia University; Tseng Ta-yu, artist-translator and instructor in Chinese calligraphy at San Francisco City College; Achilles Fang of Harvard University; Dudley Fitts, translator of Greek and Latin American poetry; William McNaughton of Oberlin; Jung-pang Lo of the University of California; Shau Wing Chan of Stanford University; F. S. C. Northrop and Norman Holmes Pearson of Yale University; C. Y. Lee, author of *The Flower Drum Song;* and John C. H. Wu of Seton Hall University.

Nor could we forget that the late St.-John Perse, William Carlos Williams and Pearl Buck were kind enough to send us words of praise and encouragement.

We are also grateful to Keith Botsford and the National Translation Center for a research grant; to Harold Graves, who printed the pamphlets from which this book in part derives; and to Shigeyoshi Murao and Fritz Maytag, who reached into their hearts and wallets to help get the pamphlets out.

We are especially grateful to Bonnie R. Crown and Zelda S. Bradburd of the Asia Society. This is one of the volumes assisted by the Asian Literature Program of the Asia Society, New York, under a grant from the National Endowment for the Humanities.

We owe further acknowledgments to *Delos* and *The Malahat Review* for permission to reprint the dialogue and translations that first appeared in their pages.

The residual errors are all ours.

C. H. K. and V. McH.

Contents

Old Friend
From Far Away

Part One

Why I Live
on the Mountain

Seeing Master Yuan Off
On His Mission to Kucha

City on Wei
          the morning rain
               wet
               on light dust
Around the inn
          green willows
          fresh
I summon you:
          drink one more cup
No old friends
when you start westward
               from Yang Kuan

WANG WEI   *T'ang*

3

After Admiring Peonies in the Chi-ch'iang Temple Garden

Old man
            unabashed
                        a flower in my hair
(but the flower
            should feel disgraced
                        up there on an old man's head)
going home drunk
            reeling on my way
                        People will laugh
But ten miles round
            the pearly blinds up
                        to see a man so gay

On the Mountain:
Question and Answer

You ask me:
              why do I live
on this green mountain?
     I smile
     No answer
                    My heart serene
On flowing water
                  peachblow
                  quietly going
                  far away
This is   another earth
           another sky
No likeness
              to that human world below

LI PO   *T'ang*

5

To the Tune of *Nü Kuan-tzu*

Last night
            at midnight
on the pillow
            I saw her!
            clear in dream
We talked
            a long time
Face the same
            like peach blossom
                Willow-
                leaf
                eyes
            often lowered
Half shy she is
half joyful
When we were
            leaving each other
                she
                clung again
Waking
        I knew—
            a dream
and the sadness
            like a pouring flood!

On Seeing Wei River
Flowing into Ch'in

Wei River
                 away eastward flowing—
when will it come to Yung-chou?
Tears add to it
                   double row
down to my village flowing

Lung Hsi Song

Took oath:
                 to sweep the Huns away or die
Five thousand soldiers gone!
                 cold fur
                 and silk
                         on alien wold
Aï! by Wu-ting River
                 bones
and the married girls
                 dreaming of them still

CH'EN T'AO   *T'ang*

Ancient Poem
(an excerpt from the *Shih Ching*)

Clever man
                erects a city
Clever woman
                  wrecks a city
Woeful thing!
               a clever woman
like an owl
            for bad omen
Woman
        has a long tongue—
ladder
      to perdition swung
Who says heaven
              sends down trouble?
Trouble's born
          of woman's hubble
These
two
    can't be taught:
           woman
           eunuch at the Court

ANONYMOUS   *Chou*

9

World's End

Spring day
                 at world's end
At world's end
                    the sun
                             declining
Heu! the nightingale
                        If there are
                        tears for me
water
                the crowns of the flowers

LI SHANG-YIN   *T'ang*

Spring Thoughts

O grass of Yen
                    like green silk flowing
Green boughs low
                      on mulberries of Ch'in
All that time!
                you've been thinking of home
and all that time!
                  my heart breaking
In my silk bedcurtain
                  spring wind
It does not know me
                Why does it come
slipping in?

LI PO *T'ang*

11

Rejoicing at Master Ch'en's Unexpected Visit

Yellow bird sings
                    and stops
Green plums
                half rounded out
I sit and grieve
                Spring's over
Then getting up
                go into the east garden for a stroll
wine cup in hand
                unwilling to drink alone
Suddenly
        a knock at the door
Even
      some ordinary caller welcome
But what a joy!
                It's Master Ch'en
Leisurely all day
                we talk:
long crowding of years
                    our feelings
                    while we were parted
Ha! never make light of
                    a cup of wine—
it can pour out
            our whole lives!

PO CHÜ-YI   *T'ang*

The War Year

Lowland hills and rivers
          dragged on to the war map
       O lowland lowlands O!
Those groaning people!
           how can they live?
              A turnip or two
              grubbed up
Don't talk to me
         about titles
           promotions
           all that slop
One general
        pulling out a victory
      leaves
          ten
          thousand
          corpses
              to rot!

TS'AO SUNG   *T'ang*

Late Spring
(written to the tune of *Wu-ling Ch'un*)

Wind stopped
           earth
           smelling of fallen blossoms
Day almost over
               Too weary to comb my hair
His belongings here
         He here no longer
                   Everything useless
Before I can say a word
               tears flow first

At Twin Stream
           they say
               the spring still beautiful
I too
     would like to go rowing in a light boat
but I'm afraid
            that little boat on Twin Stream
would not carry
         so much sorrow!

LI CH'ING-CHAO   *Sung*
14

Night Mooring at Cow's Creek:
I Think of the Old Days

At Cow's Creek
                on Western River
                                the night
Sky still blue
            not a rag of cloud
I go on deck
            to look at the bright moon
thinking of
            the great General Hsieh of old

I also
        can make poetry
but that man's like
                    will not be found again
In the morning
                we make sail and go
The maple leaves
                fall as they will

LI PO   *T'ang*
15

Impromptu on a Spring Day

Few clouds
breeze light
   coming up to noon
By flower hedge
by willow way
    I cross the neighbor stream
Friends these days
    do not know my glowing thought
They're bound to say:
    there goes the truant boy

CH'ENG HAO   *Sung*
16

Message to a Northern Friend
On a Rainy Night

You ask when I'm coming back
                              The date
                              not set yet
On Pa Shan
              night rain
                              brimming autumn pools
Ah! when shall we
              at western window
                              trim candles together
and gossip about
              tonight's rain on Pa Shan?

LI SHANG-YIN   *T'ang*

Speaking of Poetry

Judgment of poetry
                        must have root in the man
In coterie
           the arguments
                        all geese-gabble
Dwarf watching a play
                What can he see?
and what can he do
            but parrot
                   the *good!*
                   bad!
                   babble?

CHAO YI *Ch'ing*

18

Night Vigil

Incense
to ash
in bronze bowl
         Faint drop
         waterclock
Light scissory wind
            waves of chill
Spring witching
stirs me
     I can't sleep
Moon moving
      Flower shadows
              climb the balustrade

WANG AN-SHIH *Sung*

19

To the Tune of *Yi Hsien Tzu*

Feasted once
                 in deep peach glades
one song
             phoinix to phoinix
             danced and sang
I recall
        —how long!
                      saying goodbye to her
Tears mingled together
                    hand on arm to the door
          like a dream
          like a dream
faded moon
fallen blossoms
             thick mist
                  over all

Mooring on Ch'in-huai River

Mist
　　　folded over cold water
　　　　　　　　moon veil
　　　　　　　　on sandy banks
Mooring at night on Huai
　　　　　　　close by
　　　　　　　a river tavern
Flower girls
　　　　you don't know
　　　　　　　　sorrow!
　　　　　　　—a kingdom gone
still out over the river
　　　　　　shrilling indelicate songs

TU MU　*T'ang*
21

To My Younger Brother Tzu-yu:
An Excerpt

Life of man everywhere
                        You know what it's like?
A wild goose
                walking on snowy ground
On snowy ground
                        haphazard
                                    leaving tracks
The goose flies away
                    with never a care
                            which way he goes
                            or where he's going

Visiting Ch'i-an

North   of the river
south
                        myriad willows
The mountain
                front and back
                        peachbloom everywhere
Not yet
            as earthly things
                        this body passing
Each year
            I'll come to catch
                        today in spring

WANG AN-SHIH   *Sung*

To Someone Far Away

When she was here
            pretty darling
                        flowers filled the hall
Now she's gone
            pretty darling
                        left her bed behind
On her bed
                th'embroidered coverlet
                        rolled up
                        never slept in again
Three years to the day
                        still keeps
                        the scent of her
Fragrance never lost
Pretty darling
                never came back
Yellow leaves falling
                    when I think of her
white dew
            on green moss

LI PO   *T'ang*
24

Parting Gift

Much love
                —why did it seem no love at all?
Over the last bottle, nothing;
                                could not rouse a smile
The candle
                gracious enough to regret our parting
made tears for us
                Dawn came in a while

TU MU   *T'ang*

Written on a Farmhouse Wall
In a Southern Suburb of the Capital

A year ago today
                inside this door
her pretty face
the peach flowers
             each to each
             reflected pink
Pretty Face!
         where is she now?
Still the peach flowers
               crinkling
               in
               spring
               wind

TS'UI HU *T'ang*

Spring Lingering

Slowly my years
                go into dark
Worn traveler's
mourning for spring
                      only he can know
Rosy as ever
             the flowering peach after rain
but long ago
             men's hearts
                     turned to the rose

LÜ CHIANG   *Sung*

27

Recruiting Officer at Shih-hao Village

Came at dusk into Shih-hao Village
Draft officer there
                      rounding up people by night
Old man
         climbed over the wall
                   escaped
Old woman came out the door
                 staring
Officer roared
        Angry as a bull!
Old woman cried
        Enough to twist your bowels!
I heard her
        She went up and spoke to him:
'I had three sons
        'on the border at Yeh
'The first one
        'sent me a letter
'My other two sons
        'a while back
             'killed in battle
'Survivors
        'lucky to be alive at all
'The dead
        'gone for good
'There are no more men in this house
'only
        'my grandson at the breast

'His mother
                    'stayed here to look after him
'in and out of the house
                            'without a decent
                            'skirt on her legs
'I'm an old woman
                        'weak in the back
'but please! sir
                    'let me follow you
                            'when you return tonight
'hurrying to meet
                    'the draft at Ho-yang
'I'll be in time to cook
'a morning meal
                    'for the soldiers'
Night late
            Talk dwindled away
I seemed to hear
                low sobbing
At dawn
            resumed my journey
The old man alone
                    when I said goodbye to him

To the Tune of *Wang Chiang-nan*

So many sorrows!
and last night
                    in my dream
        as if
        the old days were back
                        inspecting
                        the Imperial Park
Chariots
                like a running stream
                            so many
The horses
                    curveting dragons
Moon of flowers
                    in spring wind!

To the Tune of *Tsui Kung-tzu*

Outside my door
     the dog barking
I know what it is
     My lover's here
On with my slippers
     down
     perfumed stairs
My good-for-nothing lover
      is drunk tonight

I help him into
     my silk-curtained bed
Will he take off the silk gown?
       O! O! not he
Milord is drunk
     and drunk let him be
Better that
    than sleeping alone

ANONYMOUS WOMAN POET *Five Dynasties*

To the Number One Daughter of the Wang Family
(written to the tune of *Ho Hsin-lang*)

Once we rode
                    bamboo
                    stick horses
                                        back and forth
                                        between your house and mine
Still I remember
                    curly pigtails
                    covering your neck
rouge
            dabbed on your forehead
Your mother
led you by the hand
                    Your father
                    carried you piggyback
Sometimes
            you put on boy's clothes
Though you were very small
                                        my heart
                                        hurt for you
After school
            when you got home before dark
you'd come up to my red room
                    asking:
                                        is the wild quince in bloom?
                                        have you seen a gold finch yet?
and beg me
            for a brush pen
            to paint your eyebrows

Twenty years
                    over the world
                                        a long-time wanderer
and everything that's happened
                                    like a flaw of wind
                                    passing dream
mere rain and cloud
                        dividing us
Today
            meeting again
                            in this room
we still keep—
                    shall I say?—
                                    certain affections
together with
                    some evidence of sociability
Dear lady!
            do you remember
                                    years ago
                                    when you were shy and small
it needed only a word from me
                                    to get you all worked up
and your cheeks
                    would turn
                    bright pink?
I'd give
my right eye
                to see
                        just that again!

CHENG HSIEH   *Ch'ing*
33

Answering Vice-Prefect Chang

In my later years I care for nothing but quietness
All things now
                    inconsequent to my heart
I take thought for myself
                            No splendid plans
I only know
                I'll go back to my house in the woods
Pine wind blowing
                     loosening my sash
Mountain moon
                on my hands playing the lute
You ask
          if I've construed the poles of being
Listen! a fisherman's song
                    going far up the river

WANG WEI *T'ang*

34

Part Two

The Lady
and the Hermit

華

Like Marceline Desbordes-Valmore, Notre Dame des Pleurs
*of the French, the elegant Li Ch'ing-chao of the Sung made
her poems out of the often sorrowful cycle of a woman's
life. She is regarded as the classic Chinese woman poet.*

*Wang Fan-chih of the T'ang was a Buddhist hermit who
spoke from his rough Walden a thousand years before
Rousseau at the Island of St. Peter but very nearly at the
same time as those other poets of happy hermitage, the
Irish.*

Placed together, Li and Wang make yin *and* yang *in
startling black-and-white.*

To the Air of *T'ien Tzu Ts'ai Sang-tzu*

Who
>planted the plantain tree
>>there
>>outside my window?
>*Shadow fills the court*
>*Shadow fills the court*
>>Each leaf
>>each blade
stretched
>and curling in my heart

Woeful
>on my pillow
>>hearing
>>midnight rain
>*Plip plop! lonely and sad*
>*Plip plop! lonely and sad*
>>Lover gone
>>from lady
Strange!
>to get out of bed at night
>>and listen
>>to rain

LI CH'ING-CHAO   *Sung*

37

To the Air of *Tien Chiang Ch'un*

Ride in the swing
                    over
she stands up
                    languid
                    flexing delicate hands
Multitudinous dew
                        on thin flower
a mist of sweat
                    dampens
                    her light dress through

She looks
            A stranger coming
Her stocking down
                        Gold hairpin slipped
Shyly
        she runs
and
        leaning against the door jamb
looks back
lingering
            to sniff at a green plum

LI CH'ING-CHAO   *Sung*
38

To the Air of *Chien Tzu Mu-lan Hua*

Mignonne, allons voir si la rose . . .

Bought
　　　from the flower-peddler's tray
one spring branch
　　　　　just open
　　　　　in bloom
Droplets
　　　fleck it evenly
still clouded red
　　　　with a mist of dew

I'm afraid he'll
　　　　take it into his head
that my face is not
　　　　so fair!
　　　　so fair!
In high-
combed hair
　　　I fasten
　　　　　a gold pin
　　　　　aslant
There!
let him look
　　　Let him compare the two

LI CH'ING-CHAO   *Sung*
39

Midautumn Festival
(to the air of *Tsui Hua Yin*)

Thin haze
dense clouds
                Melancholy all day long
Incense fuming
             in the bronze lion boat
Now once again
                Midautumn Festival
Through   jade pillow   at midnight
          silk screen
the creeping early chill

At east hedge
             drinking wine in the twilight
intimate perfume
               welling from our sleeves
Ah no! don't say
          all this
          is not enchantment
Curtain
       lifting in the west wind
and I
     thinner than the frailest yellow flower!

LI CH'ING-CHAO *Sung*
40

To the Air of *Tieh Luan Hua* No. 1

Long placid evening
                          my diversions few
I
     vacantly dreaming of Ch'ang-an
how the road
                     goes up
                     to the old capital
Please tell them:
                          spring
                          is fine
                          this year
Flower glow
moon shadow   set each other off

Pleasant to take   wine
                          food
                     without picking and choosing
Excellent wine
                          a tart plum
—just right for my mood
Tipsy
           I put a flower in my hair
                          O *flower! flower!*
                          don't make fun of me
Have pity!
                Spring
                like all men living
                               will soon
                               grow old

LI CH'ING-CHAO   *Sung*

Other people ride
                    great big horses
I'm the only one
                    bumping on an ass
But look!
back there
            —I feel a little better
A pack of dry sticks
                    riding on a man

WANG FAN-CHIH   *T'ang*

42

2
_____

I have land

       ten acres

on South Mountain terrace

           planted

           to rice

Green pines

       four or five trees

A few beanrows

      green

      beans

Hot

   I jump in the pool

cool

   I sing on the shore

A free man

      sufficient

      to himself

Who

   can do anything to harm me?

WANG FAN-CHIH   *T'ang*

43

3
___

All of us receive
                    an empty body
All of us
            take
            the universe's breath
We die
            and still
            must live again
come back to earth
                    all recollection lost
Ai! no more than this?
                        Think hard about it
All things turn
                stale and flat on the tongue
It comforts people? No
                        Better
                        now and again
to get blind drunk on the floor
                            alone

WANG FAN-CHIH   *T'ang*
44

4

*Whoso stoppeth his ear at the cry of the
poor shall cry himself and not be heard*

A poor man
            —don't brush him off
        or give him the go-by
Food in the house?
                By all means
                invite him in
And medicine
            to heal that sore he's got
What if he *won't*
                pay you back in pearls?
                Never mind!

WANG FAN-CHIH   *T'ang*

45

Recollections of a Dream
(written to the air of *Yu Chia Ngao*)

The lyf so short, the craft
so long to lerne . . .

Sky
              cloud
      joining   in dawn murk
              sea
Star River
              about to change
                            into a thousand
                            sails
                            dancing
So
      as if my other I
went back
              to Heaven's Emperor's House
I hear
              Heaven speak
solicitous
              asking
              where I'm going

I answer:
              'A long way
'lamenting
                '—how late in the day!
'Mastered
'the poetic art
                  'and got
'not one line
              'to startle the world'

I now
        like the Great Bird P'eng
        Wind-Rider
first
lifting wing
            on his journey
            —90,000 miles!
O wind!
hold true
        Blow my sail
far out
        to the Immortals'
        Three
        Islands

To the Air of *P'u-sa Män*

Wind soft
        late in the day
        Still early spring
The quilted vest
        put on quickly
        warms me
Waking
      I felt a slight chill
Plum blossom
        faded in my hair

My home village
        —which way
        does it lie?
Forget?
      Only one way
      —drink
Guru incense lighted
        when I went to bed
Incense
burnt out
      The wine cloud remains

LI CH'ING-CHAO   *Sung*

To the Air of *Nan Ko-tzu*

In the sky
        Star River
        winding its course
On earth
      the bamboo screen
      lowered
Chill
    rising in
         pillow and mat
      The tear stains
      grow
I'll get up
      loosen my silk jacket
and yes!
    ask
    'What time is it?'

Green
      clings to the lotus ovules
        —ah, how tiny
Bronze
      fused into the lotus leaves
        —how few
Same old weather
        same old clothes
Only my feelings
      unlike
      those I knew

LI CH'ING-CHAO   *Sung*
49

The *Wu-t'ung* Leaves
(to the air of *Yi Ch'in Wo*)

Going up
         to the high balcony
Disordered mountains
                  level plain
                  in
                  thin
                  mist
In thin mist
         the crows
         homing
I hear
      cowhorns in the dusk

Burnt-out incense
leftover wine
            Weary at heart
West wind hurrying
                wu-t'ung leaves
                to their fall
The *wu-t'ung* leaves'
              fall
      Moment of loneliness!
      Autumn sign!

LI CH'ING-CHAO *Sung*

To the Air of *Yu Meng Ling*

It comes back to me often

> River Pavilion
> sun going down

I

drowned in wine

> not knowing
> the way home

Festivities over

> start back late by boat

Confused

> I push
> deep into
> a lotus bight
> *How can I get across?*
> *How can I get across?*

and scrambling

> scare up

a whole

> flight of herons
> from the river bank

To the Air of *Feng-huang*
T'ai-shang Yi Ch'ui Hsiao

Stick incense
        cold
        in bronze lion boat
            Bedcover rumpled
            in crimson seas
Getting up listless
        I comb my hair
        alone
Neglected
        dressing table
        veiled with dust
Daybreak climbs
        the bed-curtain bar
All my life
        that dread
        in my heart
  —the bitter taste of division
So many things
        I wanted to say
        —and did not
Thinner lately
        but not from wine
        or autumn melancholy

O! O! this journey of his
And I knew
        I could not stop him

though I sang
                the Yang-kuan parting song
                a thousand times over
I think of him who is traveling
                            far away
Mist
wraps it round
                my tall house
Only the river
                flowing in front
witness
            to my daylong stare
                    and at what point
                    I stare
From now on
            each day
            will add
                        one more new grief

To the Air of *Yuan Wang-sun*

Dream broken off
                Waterclock
                still
          The sadness deepens now
             Wine
             has upset me
My cherished pillow's
                   turning cold
Jade screen
           faces
           the dawn sun
Outside my door
             who swept away
the crinkled red petals?
               That wind
               last night!

Jade flute
          stopped
        Where is he now?
         Spring!
         gone again
and he
          heartless enough
not to come home
              when he promised
      O this love!
      This grief!
      This moment!

I could commission
                    the flying clouds
to ask the God of Spring—
                    why? why? why? why?

LI CH'ING-CHAO   *Sung*

To the Air of *Tien Chiang Ch'un*

Alone
        in my inner chamber
every inch
of intestine
                bound
    in a thousand turns of woe
            Spring I love!
            and spring departing
A spat of rain
                pricks the flowers to bloom

Have I not leaned
                on every part
                of the balustrade?
        No more feeling left
        Where is he now?
Fading grasses
                blur
                into the sky
and my eyes
            go out
            to the end
                    of every
                    incoming
                    road

LI CH'ING-CHAO *Sung*

Autumnal Mood
(written to the air of *Sheng-sheng Män*)

Seeking
seeking
      Searching
      searching
over and over
             lonely and forlorn
Sighing;
grieving
sighing
      in the same round
  Now warm
  now cold
How wearisome
          to take care of myself
Two or three cups
          weak wine
—how can they fend off
            the strong wind
            that comes at nightfall?
Wild geese going over
They hurt me
        Old friends

The whole earth
         piled high
         with yellow flowers
How utterly desolate!
          For whom now
          can I pick them?

I
    watching alone
                  at the window
When will it be dark?
Wu-t'ung trees   at twilight
the fine rain
    Drip! drip!
    drop! drop!
All this
        How can
the one word *sadness*
             embrace it all?

LI CH'ING-CHAO   *Sung*
58

*My dwelling was small, and I could
hardly entertain an echo . . .*

Thatch hut's enough
> to keep out
> wind and dust

Bed?
> Not even a ragged quilt to lie on

Guests come
> I simply invite them in

Straw laid on the floor
> Mattress for sitting

No coal in the house
> Hemp stalks   make my fire
> willow twigs

White wine
> kept in earthen bowls

My old *ch'eng*
> —two legs broken off

Deer meat jerky
> three or four strips

Rock salt
> five or six little crystals

Wide-eyed
> my guests politely *oh* and *ah*

Let them
> Let them laugh at me
> as much as they like!

WANG FAN-CHIH   *T'ang*
59

6
_____

I
   saw
       that man die
my bowels
         hot as fire
not
    because I pitied the man
           Fear!
           Fear!
How do I know
         I won't be next?

WANG FAN-CHIH   *T'ang*
60

Wisdom's eye
           denotes
                    the subtle mind
not at all
         a mere
                  hole in the skull
Face to face
            you say you don't know me
but I forgive you
              though
                     your mother's name
                     is
                     KNOW*

*A pun. The character for the family name 董, pronounced Tung or Doong, was a homonym for 懂, meaning to know, to know all, to understand.

WANG FAN-CHIH   *T'ang*

8

A greedy man dies of moneymaking

Buying buying buying   farmsteads
                 estates
                   Rebuilding
                             top to bottom
                             his own house
Snatching
         every flitter of property
         from hell to breakfast
                  Still he complains
                  'Can't get enough'
Carved panels
high roofs
         Never a minute's peace
How much time
         can he spend
         in that great house of his?

WANG FAN-CHIH   *T'ang*

Building   tract houses
        country houses
                    No end in sight
What! already
        wailing voices in the hall
               —he's dead
The mourners
relatives
      Every man jack
      gets a piece of the loot
They weep, yes
        but if the truth were known
        a happy-hearted crew

WANG FAN-CHIH   *T'ang*
63

Hundred-year men?
                    None in the world
But we slave to make
                    thousand-year songs
beating out iron
                    to bar out death
Seeing,
        the ghosts
                    clap hands
                    and laugh

WANG FAN-CHIH *T'ang*

To the Air of *Hao Shih Chin*

Wind dying
         Petal fall
         heaped up
Deep-drifted
          red snow
I recall now
       When the cherry
       bursts into flower
at that very moment
            I mourn
            for spring

Much wine drunk
         Songs all sung
         my cup empty
The green lamp
       flares dimly
       dies away
Unbearable
even in dreams
        my secret grief
How can I bear to hear
      one more note
      from the mourning cuckoo?

LI CH'ING-CHAO   *Sung*
65

To the Air of *Yi Chien Mei*

Pink lotus fragrance
>   gone
>   Green reed mat
>   breathing of autumn

Lightly
>   I loosen my silk cloak

get into the little skiff
>   alone

Who among clouds
>   has mailed me
>   a letter brushed on silk?

Back comes the wild-goose answer
>   Moonlight
>   floods the house

Petals
>   falling of their own weight

Water
>   of itself flowing

One order of wish

Two
>   locales of tender sorrow

No way
>   to get rid of this yearning

Lifted from the brows
>   that moment
>   instead
>   it creeps
>   into the heart

LI CH'ING-CHAO *Sung*

To the Air of *Yung Yu Lo*

Sunset
      molten bronze
evening clouds
            marbled white jade
   Where is he?
A mist of light
           stains the willows
Plum blowing
      A flute's wail
   Spring reveries
   how much you know!
New Year's Eve
          the merrymaking festival
Serene weather—

              wind
       no   in its wake?
              rain

Friends come
         to invite me out
               horses
               traveling carts
         wine-drinking friends
I thank these
         poem-making companions

At the capital
         joyful days
In my room
       much
       time to myself

I recall
          another New Year's Eve
how I put on
          the green-feather headdress
narrow snow-white sash
                    worked
                    with gold thread
Headdress and sash
               to vie with any beauty
I
   haggard now
               wind-tangled locks
               hair
                    frosted white
                    at the temple
Too diffident
          to venture among flowers
I loiter
          under the window screen
eavesdropping
          on the talk
          and laughter
          of others

LI CH'ING-CHAO   *Sung*

To the Air of *Yu Chieh Hsing*

Wicker bed
paper screen
    Morning
       I wake
  How can I tell it all?
  my lonely desolation
Incense burnt
     the jade pot cold
My mood now
     like water
The pipe plays an air
      three times over
How truly
    the whole spirit of spring!

Light wind
sprinkle of rain
     hissing
  to start my tears
  —a thousand rows
Gone! gone!
     my apartment empty
entrails
   twisted in grief
Who now
    will lean on the balustrade with me?
I pluck a spray of flowers

but in all
             heaven or earth
no one
          now
          can give it to him!

To the Air of *Lin Chiang Hsien*

Deep the courtyard
                    Ah, how deep!
High
        chamber windows
                            often closed
Little by little   plum flower
                   willow shoot   appear
Spring!
            coming back to the Nanking trees
I grow older
            in Nanking

Moon
        rhapsodized
breeze
                        —how many times?
                    in verse
Now old
            and nothing done
Who will pity   haggard
                woebegone   me?
Light candles?
                    I never give it a thought
Romp in the snow?
                        I have no heart for it now

LI CH'ING-CHAO   *Sung*

71

To the Air of *T'an P'o Huan Ch'i Sa*

Sick now
        white hair
        sparse
        at my temples
I lie here
        watch
the waning moon
           climb
           on my window screen
Nutmeg   twigs and all
cardamon
              Water
              boiling hot
No one
       to share this tea

On my pillow
        making verses
            best
            when I'm free for it
Out of doors
        the landscape
            best
            when it rains
and all day
facing me
        —ah! how endearing
flowers
     of the cassia tree!

LI CH'ING-CHAO *Sung*

72

Part Three

Have Pity
on the Grass

華

Pity for the Farmer Conscripts

In what age
           under what king
                      no war?
Every man in war
           hopes for a sight of peace
Today
      the earth's   more bones
                  than soil
and still they come
           drafting these countrymen
           into the frontier armies!

WEI CHUANG   *T'ang/Five Dynasties*
75

'Till White Hair We'll Stay Together'

White our love
                    as snow on the mountaintop
bright bright
                    as moon between clouds
Now I hear
                    you've taken another lover
so I come to say goodbye
Today let's drink
                    gallons of wine
tomorrow part
                    down where the canal comes out
pacing
back and forth
                    along the Imperial Canal
where the water divides east
                                west
Sad and sad and very sad!
but in marriage
                    a body
                    mustn't cry
though I wish I had
                    a loving man
Till white hair grows
                    we would not part

CHO WEN-CHUN *Han*

Looking at Spring

My country in ruins
                    Hills
                          remain
                    rivers
Spring
        coming to the city
                            The grass
                            grows tall
These sad days
                even the flowers
                                    wet
                                    with dewy tears
When I grieve
                at our separation
                                    even a bird
                                    can startle me

Fighting
        goes on and on
                        these first three months
A letter from home
                    worth
                    ten thousand pieces of gold
The more I scratch my white hair
                                the shorter it gets
—almost too short
                to hold a hairpin!

TU FU   *T'ang*

Questions About a Bite

On your shoulder
plain as day
                the marks of teeth
    You tell me
    Who bit you?
I won't scold you
You can save me the trouble
                      of asking you questions
                      day after day
    What's bitten
            is your flesh
    What hurts
            is my heart
What kind
           of monster
would bite you
           with such cruelty?

ANONYMOUS WOMAN POET *Ming*
78

Ch'eng Teh Melody

A maid of Chao
                    ran off in the spring
                              and climbed a painted tower
Once she began to sing
                    her songs
                    filled the city
                              In autumn now
absently
          she sings another song
          —a song of the border fighting
and even if you were no soldier
                              you too
                              would weep at that

WANG PIAO   *T'ang*
79

Written to the Tune of *Sheng Ch'a-tzu*

Spring mountains
                              Fog
                              about to disperse
Sky clear
                    stars few
A fading moon
                              shines on your cheek
We cry at parting
                              as the day comes up

So many words!
                              but the feeling
                              strong as ever
Turning your head
to look back
                    you call
                    over and over
'Remember the Green-Skirt Girl
                              'and everywhere on earth
                              'be tender with the grass'

NIU SHI-CHI   *T'ang/Five Dynasties*
80

Winter Evening:
Rejoicing that a Friend Has Come

What
      corner of earth
      haven't you been to?
and tonight
          you're here
          in a friendly glow
Your village home
              —you've been away
              a long time
The war
      not over yet

Wicker lamp
getting dim
          still a flick'ring light
Snow
      falling heavy without a sound
What a lot of things
             you have seen and heard!
You must
      talk and talk until morning

LI HAN-YUNG *T'ang*
81

To My Husband

You
guard the border pass
                    I
                    live at Wu
The autumn gales
blow over me
                    I
                    worry about you
every line
of my letter
                    a thousand rows of tears
Has the cold
reached you there?
                    Did you get
                    the clothes I sent you?

CH'EN YU-LAN   *T'ang*

On Not Seeing Li Po

I have not seen
>> Master Li
>> this long time
His pretended madness
>> —what a truly pitiable thing!
The whole world
>> wants to be rid of him
I alone
>> cherish his talent
So nimble-witted
>> he can write
>> thousands of poems
forced to walk the roads
>> drinking country wine
On K'uang Shan
>> his old study
 —when his hair is white
>> it might be best
>> to go back there

Under the Moon: Drinking Alone

per amica silentia lunae

Flowers all round
                    One pot of wine
Solitary
           drinking without a friend
I raise my cup
               to invite
               the bright moon
With my shadow
                   we make three:
the moon
             —though it doesn't know how to dance
and my shadow
                 —which can only follow me
For the moment
               I'll make do
               with moon and shadow
Enjoyment
           is fitting
           to the spring
I sing
       and the moon
       wavers to and fro
I dance
       and my shadow
       gets all mixed up
Sober
      we frolic together
Drunk
       each goes his way alone

We three
           forever-silent friends
will meet some day
                    in the clouds up above

Night: I Climb on the City Wall
And Hear a Flute Playing

Under Hui-lo Mountain
                    the sands
                    like snow
Outside the city wall
—surrendered by the enemy
                         the moon
                         like frost
Who can tell
            where that blowing of a flute
            comes from?
All night long
            the soldiers long for home

To the Tune of *Chien Tzu Mu-lan Hua*

Nobody
      bothers about me
I alone
      take good care of myself
Independent as all hell
refusing
      to follow others
I
  go my own way alone

The universe
      so vast
yet still
    they choose to sit
      on the sharp points
      of needles and thorns
I
  as in the old days
        embrace emptiness
        sleep till dawn

CHU TUN-YU   *Sung*
87

Reading the Ancient Classic:
Hills and Seas

Early summer
                    grasses and plants tall
Around my house
                    trees are flourishing
All sorts of birds
                    happy
                    finding a place to rest
I too
        delight in my poor cottage
Ploughing done
                    seeds in the ground
sometimes
                    I get a chance
                    to read my books
In the narrow lane
                    deep ruts
                    far apart
Often
            they turn back
            my friends' carriages
Happily I drink
                    the spring wine
pick
        my garden vegetables

Light rain
                    from the east

A good breeze
                    comes with it
I pore over
                    King Chou's story
glancing at pictures
                              in the ancient classic
                         Hills and Seas
Up and down
                    I gaze at heaven and earth
Not happy?
                    How could I be otherwise?

Poem Written to an Old Tune

My love
           goes home at night
                        How goes the night?
Moon shining
              We part at the door
Two nights later
                    I wait for his coming
open the door
              There's only the bright moon

HO CHU *Sung*

To the Tune of *Sheng Ch'a-tzu*

You
      like dust in the road
I
   like willow catkins
   along the dike
When we two met
         so light we were
even our footprints
       couldn't be found

Your face
glowing with wine
       as if chafed
       by spring wind
My tear-filled eyes
       as if autumn rain
       were falling
Now that we've said goodbye
do you still
     have yearnings for me?

YAO K'UAN *Sung*

91

To the Tune of *Pu Suan-tzu*

Wanting to see him
                    I can't see him
Wanting to be near him
                        I can't get near him
I ask you
            How much loving
            do I get from him?
    More perplexed
    than annoyed
I can't hold back
                    can't stop the tears
can't help
            feeling bad
In heaven and earth
                    there are sorrows
    but this one
    I understand
    all too well!

HUANG T'ING-CHIEN *Sung*

A Beauty

In the North Country
                              a beautiful lady
Paragon of the age
                    she stands alone
One smile from her
                          would bring down a city
two smiles
              tumble a nation
Ha! don't I know
                      she can ruin
                      city or nation?
Such a beautiful lady
                          I will not find again!

Sent to My Husband

In sleep
           I see you returning
Awake
           I cannot see your face
I
   send you my picture
Morning and night I
                  will be
                  beside you

A Poem

You
        come from my village
You ought to know
                        what goes on
                        in our part of the world
The day you left
                —outside
                my silk-paned window
that winter plum
                —was it blooming yet?

Written to the Tune of *P'u-sa Män*

Flowers glowing
           dim moonlight
               sky
               veiled in light mist
O what a night
           to go to my lover
In stocking feet
           tiptoe
           down fragrant stairs
hands holding
           gold threaded shoes

South of the Painted Hall
                 meeting my lover
for a moment
           I lean against him
           trembling
'I want you
           '—because it's so hard to come here at all
'I want you
           'to love me as hard as you can!'

PRINCE LI YU   *Southern T'ang*
96

Returning to Chiang Village

Lofty red clouds in the west
Sun
    well down on the plain
A wooden door
         Noisy twitter of birds
The traveler's back
          from thousands of miles away
Wife
children amazed
       that I'm still alive
When they get over the shock
          they cry
          and wipe away the tears
In time of war
     forced
     to wander about
I return alive
    only by chance
The neighbors
     all come out along my wall
They are moved
     and sigh
     Weep too
Late that night
     we light candles again
facing each other
     like people in a dream

TU FU *T'ang*
97

Written to the Tune of *Che-ku T'ien*

Once
        because of the plum blossoms
                I got drunk
                stayed out all night
A pretty one
        tugged at my sleeve
        begging a new poem
Delicate rouge
         —I scribbled
        all over a bridal scarf
Dark-green wine
         —girls fought
        to pour it in my jade cup

Now
     I'm already old
and everything's changed
No more
        drinking with flower girls
                Tears
                wet my gown
Now all I want
        is to close the door
        sleep
let the plum petals
        whirl away like snow!

CHU TUN-YU *Sung*

To the Tune of *P'u-sa Män*

Across the pillow
                    a thousand pledges
Our love will not end
                        till green mountains crumble
till iron weights
                float on water
till the Yellow River
                goes dry
                to the very streambed!
till Orion shows
              in broad day
till Sagittarius turns
                his arrow to the south!
Our love
        will never end
until
    at midnight
             the sun comes up!

ANONYMOUS WOMAN POET   *T'ang*
99

Wu-t'ung Shadows

A waning moon
                    slants down
Autumn wind
                    cold
Tonight my lover
                    —*will he come*
                    or won't he?—
keeps me standing
                    a long time
                    in the *wu-t'ung* shadows!

ANONYMOUS WOMAN POET   *T'ang*

Liang-Chou Song

Grape wine
                prime
                        in crystal cups
but just as we start in to drink
                                the *p'i-p'a* sounds
                                to horse again
Aï! if we lie
                drunk on the battlefield
                do not mock at us
Since ancient times
                        how many men
                                        who went into battle
                                        ever came back?

WANG HAN   *T'ang*

Written to the Tune of *Pu Suan-tzu*

I
   live at the riverhead
you
      at the mouth
Every day
        I long for you
        and can't see you
though together
          we drink
          from the same river

River water
        —when will it run dry?
My sorrow
        —when will it end?
I only hope
        that your heart's
        like my heart
Surely then
        you will not fail
        my long
          love for you

LI CHIH-YI *Sung*

Domestic Scene

Plum blossoms in pots
                              a few open
                              perfume filling the room
I stare at them
                    forgetting everything else
When I chance to go into
                            the inner house
                                      my daughter
                                      thinks it odd
and asks me
                  'Why does your gown
                  'smell so good?'

Listening to Rain
(written to the tune of *Yu Mei-jen*)

When I was a youth
　　　　　　listening to rain
　　　　　　in a singsong house
red candles at dusk
　　　　　　silk bedcurtains
Then I was a man
　　　　　　listening to rain
　　　　　　in a packet boat
river wide
clouds low
　　　　scattered wild geese
　　　　crying in the autumn gale

Now
　　　listening to rain
　　　　　　　　on the cloister roof
hair at my temple
　　　　　　　so soon! patched with white
Sorrow/joy
　　　　　　no feelings at all!
parting/reunion
Let the rain
　　　　drip on my doorstep
　　　　until morning comes

CHIANG CH'IEH　*Sung*
104

Farewell

Seeing my lover off
                        on Tan Yang Road
He weeps
            I weep too
The driver
               also weeps
'Driver
           'why do you weep?'
He answers
'The gentleman who is leaving
                            'can't bear
                            'to part with you
'You, lady
              'keep blubbering away
'The two of you
                 'dawdle on and on
'and all the time
                'my donkey
                'is suffering!'

ANONYMOUS WOMAN POET *Ming*
105

My House on Chung-nan Mountain

Middle age
        is very like the Tao
Lately
        I've made my home on the mountainside
Many times
          when I take the notion
          I wander off alone
Wonderful things
            that only I know
I walk
       till I come to the head of a brook
sit down
         and watch the clouds beginning to rise
If I happen to meet
             some old coot in the woods
we chatter and laugh
           and forget to go home

WANG WEI   *T'ang*
106

Part Four

The Good-for-Nothing Lover:
A Cycle of Ming
Dynasty Folk Songs

He's the lowest man that I ever seen . . .

1

My good-looking lover

                  my good-for-nothing

I treat you

        like   gold

               jade

You treat me

         like   dirt

                mud

Up until now

          it's come out

          just as they said it would

The silly one

         is I

The heartless one's

              you

There are people who say

                     I'm wrong

There are also

          people who say

          you

          are wrong!

2

Poor little me!
                I push the window open
just to look at
               stars
               in the sky
and right off
               my mother says
               'You're carrying on
                      with someone'
Even
        the tapeworm in my belly
                   didn't get the news
                   so fast!
I suspect
        my mother's
        been through all this before!

3

I hate wind
                playing with the willow branches
                      making shadows
                      at my windows
It wakes me up
                I push my pillow
                out of the way
                            jump up
and ask 'Who is it?'
I ask again
              thinking
                  'Very likely
                  'my good-for-nothing lover
                  'has come'
But everything's quiet
                      No one answers
I
   shut up
   in a hurry
laughing at myself
                      for being such a fool
Now I'm even
                letting the wind
                scare me out of my wits

4

Against the law
                to be sleeping with me?
                Don't worry, darling
If we're caught
          doing it
          I'll
                take the blame myself
Even if
      they bring me
      before the magistrate
kneeling
        both knees
        swollen like puddings
I'll confess
        the whole thing
        from the first
and even if
        they condemn me
          to eat nails
          and chew iron bars
I'll say
      'It was all my fault
          '*I* seduced *you*'

5

What shall I say you're like?
    Like sea foam
                    You appear
                    and disappear
Like a spider's web
                    You entangle
                    the innocent
Like a spool of thread
                        You tie things up
                        for a little while
Like a flying kite
                    You're
                    the broken string
Like a carrying pole
                        You can't
                        catch your balance
                            or lift
                            a load
Shall I compare you
                        to a colored lantern
                        at New Year's?
You can't
            get all lighted up
            for three or four nights
            in a row!

You want to leave me?
>   Wait!
>   until sky
>   changes to earth

You want to leave me?
>   Wait!
>   until east
>   becomes west

You want to leave me?
>   Wait!
>   until governors
>   turn into clerks

Part with you?
>   Yes!
>   but I can't
>   part with you

Though I die
>   and go down
>   to the Land of Death

even my ghost
>   will not
>   be parted from you!

I want
       to write
       a love letter
but I can't
          I can't write
Bother someone
             to write it for me?
—no no!
        that won't do
Helpless
        I draw a few circles
        signs
This letter's
        for my love
        that he may know
        my thought
Single circle
          meaning me
Double circle
          meaning him
But I can't tell him
            all my miseries
All I can do
        is keep drawing circles
        over and over
All I can do
        is keep drawing circles
        over and over

8

My good-looking lover!
                         My good-for-nothing!
Why
        do you listen to gossips?
                         You want to leave me?
                         For good?
If you
         decide to leave me
that very minute
                         I'll get a rope
                         and hang myself
If you die
            I'll die too
We'll cross
            the Bridge to the Land of Death
            together
But if
        after five hundred years
                         our spirits
                         come back to earth
O! but I'll still
            want to make up with you!

My good-looking lover
                    my good-for-nothing
drinks
          until he's stoned
When I help him in
                    he falls on my bed
                    north/south
any old way
                    east/west
Who
        could have done this?
          May Heaven strike
          whoever it was
                              that tricked him
                              into getting blind
My poor friend!
                    he never was
                              any good
                              at holding his liquor
Why do they keep
                    pushing it on him
                    like this?
If he really gets sick
                    from all this drinking
I don't care
                    if they give me
                              ten other men
                              It won't do!

My good-looking lover
I told you
          never
          to drink yourself silly again
so how is it
now today
          you've managed to get
          boiled as an owl?
And your drinking companion?
I can imagine
          Some sing-song girl
Nevertheless
          I forgive you
but you also
          must think it over
          two or three times
If she means to treat you
          with any
          real love
how could she
          bear the thought
          of getting you drunk?

My good-looking lover!

My good-for-nothing!

You and I

once

swore a pact

but even

before our   blankets

pillows

are cold

you're

bad-mouthing me to others

Why is this?

I think it's because

your sweet honeyed words

are all

pretenses

Though I know clearly

you're fickle-minded

I know

you're cheating on me

in the end

I can only stamp my foot

beat my breast

let out a long sigh

Regret?

I should regret

getting mixed up with you

in the first place

Blame?

    I *blame nobody but myself*
    I *blame nobody but myself*

My good-looking lover
　　　　　　　my good-for-nothing
I've treated you
　　　　　　like a bronze mirror
Up until now
　　　　　I've polished you bright
　　　　　to give light to others
Now you go hand-in-hand with her
　　　　　　　　　　leaving me alone
We may know someone
　　　　　　　　but not his face
We may know his face
　　　　　　　but not his heart
In front of me
　　　　　you're nice as pie
In front of me
　　　　　you're nice as pie
but behind my back
　　　　　　　you're spineless as a worm

Idling
          alone under the moon
thinking of my lover
thinking
                of my good-for-nothing lover
O moon goddess
please!
          help me
          Witness
that *I bore him*
                    a true and faithful love
I bore him
                a true and faithful love
and he
          —he was false to me!

When you
          get mad with me
I look at you
               pretending to giggle
When you hit me
               I let you
I make believe
               we're just playing
When you bawl me out
                    I listen
as if
     you were calling me *darling*
I love you
          to scold me
          It sounds so good
I love you
          to hit me
               You do it
               so gracefully
I still love you
               happy or angry
               I don't care
These things
          all feel
          so wonderful to me!

15

Clay figurines
look as much alike
                        as we two
Mold one
            like you
Mold one
            like me
Take a look at them
                        side by side
then crumble them up together
                        and start over
Again make
            another you
Again make
            another me
In my figurine
            there's some part of you
In your figurine
            there's some part of me!

My good-looking lover
                    my good-for-nothing
You
        load me with easy promises
        no feeling at all
Haven't I always
                        been straight with you?
                        Straight from the heart!
But you
            like a bamboo broom
sweep me
                right out of your life
Flowers falling
                    still leave
                    a shadow behind
but in water flowing
                        no true
                        affection remains
You! You!
                of all the people in the world
the meanest one
                    is you!

17

Many a time
                    I've wanted to hit you
—and don't you believe for a minute
                                    I'm only fooling
I grit my teeth
I really
            want to beat you
so you won't dare
                        to bully me
But just
            as I'm going to hit you
I go
        all funny inside
and think it over a while
If I just
            hit you a little
you won't
                be afraid of me
If I really
                give you a clout
—but I wouldn't
                    have the heart
                    to do that to you
Oh! let it go
                    my good-for-nothing lover
I'd just as soon
                not hit you at all!

18

My good-looking lover
                    my good-for-nothing
Yesterday
in front of my parents
                    he promised to marry me
                    We even set the date
He swore
he would come tonight
                    after dark
                    and meet me at my house
Now
        the night's late
people in bed
Why
        don't I see him coming?
I watch the moon
                    climbing over
                    the rose trellis
He tricked me
                    into leaving my bedroom door
                    half open
Now I stare
                    vacant at the moon
straining
                    my eyes for him
without even
                    getting a glimpse
                    of his shadow

I hate
  that good-for-nothing louse!
He sneaks away
   and makes a fool of me!
He sneaks away
   and makes a fool of me!

My good-looking lover!
                    My good-for-nothing!
because of you
I'm suffering all the time
                    Everybody's
                    laughing at me
In the end
            I can only
            swallow my pride and be silent
In front of people
behind their backs
what do I get?
                    Jeers
                    even from my own family
all round me
I'm hemmed in by them
spoiling
            all my plans
No way
            I can speak out
                        I can't
                        explain
only
        be shy
                    and bow my head
good or bad
right or wrong
I've suffered it all
                    for *my good-for-nothing lover*

People
       just ha-ha-ha at me!
People
       just ha-ha-ha at me!

Wind O!
          Wind O!
I beg of you
               Stop blowing
Wind bells!
               Wind bells!
You!
     I hate you now
You
     and your everlasting
     ting-a-linging
     under the eaves
I
   never used to
   hear you at all
Now who is it
                 stirs you up
knowing
          I'm lonely?
Wind!
        you're playing
        tricks on me

Anguished
        lovesick
so woebegone
        I don't know
        what I'm doing
Tea?
    I don't think of it
Rice?
     I don't think of it
Wine?
     Too listless
     to take a sip
I'm like
       some perfectly sensible person
          who's got
          into a trap
My mouth says
     'Get rid of him!'
but my heart says
      'I still love him!'
and just as soon
as I say
    'Get rid of him!'
it turns out
     I yearn for him
     more than ever!

Thanks to you
my good-for-nothing lover

                        I've gotten sick
                        and skinny as a rat

Thanks to you
my good-for-nothing lover

                        I'm always
                        down in the mouth

When we meet each other

                        I hold your hand

O to die

               under peony blossoms

and turn into
pure spirit

                  So romantic!

To go down

                   to the Land of Death

But even then
my tricky darling

                    I'll never let go of your hand!

23

You
      boarding a boat
                    on your way home
about
      to part with me
and it gets me
           all upset
I'm afraid
      of losing you
Can't help it
      I cry hot tears
      I'm feeling so bad
Now
      it's beginning
Old love
      —when will we
           be back
           together again?
New sorrow
      —when will it end?
Though my body's locked
         behind heavy doors
my heart
      still follows
      wherever you go

Green mountains
                    here
blue waters
                here
My good-for-nothing lover
                            not here!
Often
        a breeze comes up
often
        the rain comes
His love letters
                never come!
Disasters?
                Don't harm me
Sickness?
                Can't touch me
But often
            the thought of him
            hurts me
Spring gone
                My sorrows
                do not go
Flowers bloom
                    My sadness
                    undispersed
Leaning
            against the doorframe
hand to cheek

I think of him
          and the tears
          come down in floods
filling up
     the Eastern Sea
          filling up
          the Eastern Sea

My good-looking lover's
                    gone away
                    leaving me bitter lonely
We agreed
            when   peach   flowers bloomed
                   plum
            he
                 would start back to me
I
    stare at   fish in the river
               wild geese on the shore
Never seeing
always sorrowing for   a letter
Many a twilight
                 whiled away
scratching up
            the beautiful
            carved balustrades
He! he seems like
                a kite
                that's broken its string
and never again
                will show
                even an edge
                of shadow!

I think of you, lover
        think
        think
                till my head goes round
I call the maid
'Bring me a brush pen'
        I'll draw
                        your manners
                        and the little ways you have
But I can't draw
                        your wild
                        love for me
I can't draw
                        my wild
                        love for you
I can only draw
                        the two of us
                        making love
I stop the brush
                        and think
        think
        think
                till I'm frightened
Then I draw and draw
                        like mad

But I can't draw
                    your passion
I can't draw
              your passion
              Lover!
                          I can only
                          burn for you

Last year's grasses
                    green
                    over the fields again
            apricot
Last year's   again
            peach
                        clustering
                        on the branch
Last year's swallows
                        just coming back again
Last year's azaleas
                    once again in bloom
Last year's weeping willows
                            droop
                            their slender fronds again
Why is it then
                from the one
                who went away
last year
        no news
                    not even
                    a single piece of paper?

My good-looking lover
              my good-for-nothing
No word from you
              since you went away
Often
        I've wanted
        to draw your picture
but time and again
              my brush comes down
              and I make a mess of it
Easy enough
              to draw
              the way you look
but that black heart of yours
                        is hard
                        to catch
I happen to drop
              a blob
              of black ink
There!
        that's the very image
        of your heart!

You
     send me a letter here
I cry a little
          even before I open it
remembering how
         in the beginning
         we walked hand-in-hand
stood side-by-side
sat
     slept together
my only trouble
         in dreams
         that we might be parted
Who could have guessed
           how today would be
how I'd wait
       for this one letter?
Even if you wrote me
         a thousand letters a day
they could never
       take the place of you!

30

Skyful of stars
                    no light
                    like the bright moon
Can a flock of crows
                        outshine
                        a single phoinix?
My new lovers?
                    No match
                            for the old
                    That good-for-nothing bastard!
So rare
            you could comb the world
            for his like
Among my wooers
                        he's still
                        Number One
By my side now
                    there are
                    new lovers
but in my heart
                    I
                    still yearn for him!

Part Five

The Drinking Man
the General
and Others

*The Drinking Man is of course Li Po, though the sobriquet
might fit almost any Chinese poet, or poet. The General is
Hsin Ch'i-chi, a general indeed — 'a national hero,' as Teng
Kuang-ming writes — and a great insurrectionary leader of
the Northern Sung against the invading Tatars. Out of the
wreck of a betrayed army he led ten thousand cavalry down
into the Southern Sung. But the politicos distrusted him and
Hsin spent most of the rest of his life in involuntary
retirement, an old warrior importuning the throne with
such counsels as Ten Memorials on Resisting the Tatars.
Some 620 of his poems have been saved, many of them in
the style of his superbly versatile and luminous tz'u.*

Che-ku T'ien

*In time all haggard hawks
will stoop to lure ...*

In my youth
     ten thousand men
          came to my banners
quick cavalry
     in brocade coats
          crossing the Yangtze
Night
     the north men
          stacking quivers
          worked with silver
Morning
     the south men
          letting go
          their brass-tipped arrows

Musing over bygone things
I
   sigh at my present state
Never spring wind
          will turn
          this white beard black again
and instead of my
          ten-times-ten
          thousand-word memorials
            re
            Destroying the Tatars

what do I read?
My eastern neighbor's handbook:
How
to
Plant
Trees

Ch'ing P'ing Yueh: Passing a Night Alone in Wang's Temple on Po Shan

Starved rats
                    patter round my bed
bats
        flittering at the lamp
On the roof
                pine wind
                blowing hard
                                quick rain
            Torn windpaper
                            talking to itself

All my life
                        north
            journeying
                        south
Going home now
                    white-headed
                    long in the tooth
Under cotton quilt
                    autumn night
                                I wake
    seeing   rivers
            mountains
                    out to the ends of the earth

Coming in Through the Barrier

Clouds of Lung
         unbroken
         low
O Yellow River
         moaning as it goes!
The Barrier Mountains
            How many miles of road
joining together
         how many layers of sorrow?

Ancient Poem of Devoted Love

First winter moon
                          Cold weather's coming
North wind
               How hard I'm shivering!
I, a person of much sorrow
                        know
                        how the night drags on

Raising my head
                  I gaze
                      at the many stars
                      speckled in heaven
On the fifteenth
                  bright moon
                  full
On the twentieth
                   moon
                   beginning to wane

A traveler
               coming from a far country
gave me
          a single scroll
At the top
             it said
             'Always I long for you'
At the bottom
               it said
               'How long we have been parted!'

I put the letter
                    in the folds of my dress
For three years
                    the words
                    did not fade
I clutch
          this small memento to my heart
fearing
          that you may be
                              beyond knowing

ANONYMOUS   *Han*

Mourning the Wineshop Owner Mr. Tai

. . . quhill thain is gude wyne to sell

Old Man Tai
        down there
        in Yellow Springs
must be
     still brewing
     his Big Spring brand
On the Dark Terrace
          no Li Po
          Who's he selling
               his wine to now?

LI PO   *T'ang*
153

Leaving Po Ti City at Dawn

Dawn
      Leaving Po-ti
             high up
             in colored cloud
Back down
        before dark
              to faraway Chiang-ling
Endless
      howling of gibbons
              from both cliffs
my light boat
        moving through
              a thousand gorges

Answering the Hu-chou Magistrate
Of Hindu Ancestry Who Asked Who I Was

Call me
        Green Lotus
        Buddha's man
                angel
                cast out of paradise
hiding his name
           for thirty years
                      in the wineshops
What makes you ask
           O Hu-chou magistrate?
Don't you know
           I'm the Palingenesis
                    of the Buddha
                    of Golden Grain?

LI PO   *T'ang*
155

Casual Song to the Tune of *Chiang Er Shui*

O Westron winde, when will thou blow

Lover!
        don't make sail in the boat
        just yet
The western wind
                is making up again
Why don't you
           come home with me
           as you always do?
Lover!
        if you want anything
        please tell me
If my love's
           body's cold
           my body's warm
Why don't we be happy
                  for the moment
                  this one night
                  as long as we can?
Tomorrow
           when the wind's gone down
you can
        start on your journey
My heart
        will be at peace

FENG MENG-LUNG   *Ming*
156

To the Tune of *Sheng Chia-tsu*

Brook
      reflects my shadow
      as I walk
Sky
    at the bottom
    of the clear stream
In the sky
      rambling clouds
Among
     the rambling clouds
     am I

Lonely I sing
         Who answers me?
From hollow valley
          one echo
          clear
No ghost
     and no
     immortal angel
Peach flower
        singing in the stream

HSIN CH'I-CHI   *Sung*
157

To the Tune of *T'ang To Ling*

Wonderful views
                vie with each other
                at Ch'ing Ming Festival
Mild breeze
        just lightly
        brushing my face
With   small winecups
       plates   we assemble
             on the campagna
Ride in the palanquin? No
            She refuses
            to get in
She insists
       Everybody must walk

She sets out
       with a light step
While we walk along
          she laughs and laughs
but her phoinix-'broidered shoes
            are wearing down
            at the heel
and all at once
she leans on someone
         and laughs
         making a face
'Ow-wow! it's true
       'My feet
       'are hurting!'

HSIN CH'I-CHI   *Sung*

Mountain Life: A Happening

Moaning/moaning
                    the treetop gale
Dogs on the mountain
                    barking night and day
I shout to the houseboy
                'Open
                'the wooden gate'
Only bright moonlight
                    dazzling on the stream

WU K'UEI   *Ming*
159

The Girls of Yuen

1

In Ch'ang-kan
                the girls of Wu
Brows
eyes   dazzling
                    moon
            as
                    stars
Wooden clogs
            on feet
            like frost
You'll never catch *them*
            wearing
            crow's-head stockings!

2

Many the white-skinned
                  girls of Wu
who love to frolic
              Rocking the boat
and rolling their eyes
            to show
            how amorous they are
they
      break off flowers
              to tease
             the passing traveler

3

Lotus-picking girls
                on Yeh rivers
when they spy a traveler
                sing
                and pull back their boats
giggling
                in among the lotus flowers
Pretending to be shy
                they
                refuse to come out

4

From Tung-yang
                the white-ankled girls
From Kuei-chi
                the white-boat men
Into each other's eyes
they stare
                just as the moon's
                about to set
Plainly they must be
                touched in the head

5

Mirror Lake water's
                like the moon

Yeh River girls
                    like the snow
New gowns
            reflected
            in the clear waters
Two pictures
            O so rare

Sudden Rain

All of a sudden
                    rain
                    brooks roaring
Mist cool
              tree colors darkening
I don't know where
                          the monastery is
until suddenly
              it sends out
                          a bonging of bells
                          all round me

NI CHIA-CH'ING *Ming*
163

Climbing the Phoinix Terrace in Nanking

Atop
      this Phoinix Terrace
      phoinixes once preened
Phoinixes
         gone now
         the terrace empty
            Only the river
            flowing on below
Inside Wu Palace
           weeds bury
           deserted paths
Chin courtiers
         now
         a mound of dust
Three Peaks
       half-lost
       in blue sky
White Egret Islet
          parting
          river water
Now floating clouds
            obscure the sun
The capital
       Ch'ang-an
       —I can't see it
        and the sadness
        comes over me

LI PO *T'ang*
164

Ancient Poem

One man's life
                does not last a thousand years
but he bears
                troubles enough for a thousand
Day
      regrettably short
                      Night long
Why don't we
           hold up
           a lighted candle
                        and stroll out
to be merry?
             Now's the time
How can we
           wait for the future?
Only the fool
         loves money
and becomes
           a laughingstock
           to later ages
True
      there was once
                  Prince Wang
                  who became an immortal
but it's hard to hope
                for another like him!

ANONYMOUS   *Han*

In the Mountains

Traveling back and forth
                    I meet
                    no one
my hut
            deep in the mountains
A lone crane
                starts up with a rush
                in front of me
the draft he makes
                    stirring trees
                    in the moonlight

The Lady's Grievance
(written to the tune of *Yu Meng Ling*)

Who comes with me
                        to the bright window
                        where I sit alone?
My shadow and I
                    only
                    the two of us
When the lamp burns out
                            and I'm going to sleep
even my shadow
                    leaves me
    What shall I do?
    What shall I do?
O what a
            woebegone
creature am I!

Kiangnan Song

Comes a stranger
                    from Chao-yang
mooring
            by night
            at Chinwai River mouth
No one knows
                    what dialect he speaks
but hearing it
                the children
                clap hands

What I Saw Going on in My Mountain Garden
(written to the tune of *Ch'ing Ping Yueh*)

Cloud-high my   pines
                 bamboos
From now on
            I close accounts
            in all worldly matters
                 I'm content
Leaning on a staff
            at my mountain neighbor's gate
            I collect
                 the festival meats
White wine
         at bedside
         freshly brewed

A westerly gale's
            blowing   pear   trees
                    prune
            in my mountain garden
Some village boys
            with long poles
            stealing the fruit
Don't
     send someone
     to scare them away
This old codger
            likes to watch them
                 quietly relaxed
                 in his joy

HSIN CH'I CHI   *Sung*

Inviting Liu Shih-chiu

Green-colored wine
                        new batch
my little red-clay stove
                             and the dusk falling
Sky
        coming on to snow
Why not
            come and have
            a drink with me?

Eastern Ch'an Monastery

Pines
    filling the whole courtyard
    with wind
Bean pods
     making the fence green
I listen
    No sound of carts
                 horses
Sometimes
    there's a dharma master
    living here

LI SHENG *Ming*

To the Tune of *Ho Hsin-lang*

What a disaster!
                    I'm old
regretting
            the friends of a lifetime
            so few
And today
                how many left?
White hair
            useless
                        hanging down
                        a mile long
I laugh
        at the human world's
        innumerable busynesses
You ask
            what then
            can make me joyful
Seeing green hills!
                        how ravishing they are
and expecting
                those green hills
                to return the compliment
because
        our feeling of age
        our craggy looks
                        are much the same

Winecup in hand
                    scratching my head
                    at eastern window
I imagine
                Tao Yuan-ming
                finishing his friendship poem
in much the spirit
                    of mine today
Those
        who go scrambling after fame
—how can they know
                        the joys
                        of drinking cheap wine?
I don't regret
                the ancients
                I can't see
I regret
        that the ancients
                            can't see
                            lunatic me!
Who
        understands me?
Perhaps
            only a few

A Quatrain to Express My Feelings

By my own hand
           planted
                   these peach trees
                          plum
No need to ask
           who owns them
But this old countryman's walls
                     low
                     like his house
Nothing will do
           the spring wind
                   but to go bullying
                   my trees
In the night
           it broke off
           several sprigs of blossom

TU FU   *T'ang*
174

To the Tune of *Yang-liu Chih*

Spring going
       coming

                springs
                following each other
Winter
summer forever coming back
Moon waxing and renewed again
      waning
Time's burden
                pressing on us all

In the courtyard
                seeing only
                the ageless moon
    forever there
    forever in being
we
    do not see
                in the house
                the hundred-year man
who must turn
                in the end
                to fine dust

ANONYMOUS   *T'ang*

Up on the Mountain:
I Give This to My Students

By the brook I sit
                      watching
                      the water flow
Running stream   both at peace
my heart
Unnoticed
                the mountain moon's
                come up
pine shadows
                    mottling my gown

WANG SHOU-YEN *Ming*
176

Folk Song

Green sprig of a youth!
                    knowing no shame
you
        go walking past my front door
        and keep turning your head
My husband
                has big rolling eyes
                and he's no fool
If you want to gape at me
                        why don't you
                        come round
                        to the back door?

ANONYMOUS *Ming*
177

Giving Way to My Sad Feelings

Night long
                        where are you
                        recreant lover?
Since you stopped writing
my perfumed chamber
                                    closed
brows
            in a knot
Moon now
                        beginning
                        to drop down the sky
How can you bear
                        to stay away from me?
So I bewail
                        my single blanket
Here
            take my heart
            to be
            your heart
Then you will know
                        how much
                        I think of you!

KU CHING   *T'ang*
178

Early Summer

Cut chives
        salt leeks
                corn
                to make a paste
Fresh-cooked wheat meal
                    Its fragrance
                    fills the village
This gentleman
        who's been getting drunk
                    goes riding
                    a brown cow
north
      on the roads
east
                enjoying
                the village shows

TU YU *Sung*

Teasing
(written to the tune of a foreign song)

Peonies
         wet with dew
                      like pearls
                      the real thing
A pretty girl
             breaking one off
                strolls out
                to the front courtyard
and smiles
          asking her lover
'Is the flower
            'prettier
            'than my face?'

The lover
         meaning to tease her
says
     'Yes! The flower's prettier'
At which
         in a burst
         of girlish rage
she
    crumples the flower to bits
                       and flings them
                       at him

ANONYMOUS   *T'ang*

Li Po's Grave

By Tsai-shih River
Li Po's mound
                        among unending
plains of grass
                    rolled out
                        to a sky
                        floating with clouds
Aï! here
                under unsown fields
his bones
                    whose verses once
astonished heaven
                        and shook the earth
God knows
                    we poets
                    have no luck
but none, master
                        had
                        so bad a time as you

PO CHU-I   *T'ang*
181

Thoughts of Chairman Wen Ch'ang:*
A Translators' Dialogue

It is obviously of importance to avoid saying kuei kuǒ *"your diabolical country" instead of* kuèi kuo *"your honorable country".* . . .

AXIOM : YOU ARE THE UTTER SERVANT OF THE POET

How to translate, especially from the Mandarin? That a choice must be made, *a priori* and all the way. For us there's only one. Get it into English as nearly as possible what the man said.

And if other people think a foreign poem is a mere launch pad for their own rockets? Well, every man to his *goût,* even if it's poi. Our *goût* is the sense that we owe it to the poet to put him over into English, if we can, with not even a fingernail mangled.

How much is this mixed up with what we all learned from Pound about hard, unsquidgy language? A lot, maybe. And with the sense that all good art is indelibly personal? All—even Sophocles? Even the King James translators? Yes. And that this personal authenticity is the best possible bet that it will be truly social? No paradox. Humanity is a man.

And *not* a feeling about property rights in a poem. Simply that a man's got a right to the integrity of what he gives out under his name and seal.

V.MCH.: Well, what *do* we think? If a translator's so big-arsed he's got to horn in with his little ego, for God's sake let him go and write a poem of his own? But there's more to it than that, huh?

C.H.K.: *Yes. Yes. All kinds of good poems. "Adaptations."*

---

*Chinese God of literature now underground.

Pastiche. Think of Pound again. Of course a poet ought to say where he got it, but —

V.MCH.: Yes. That's what I feel too. And hell, it's not a *moral* problem. The Americans! Suppose there *is* a little cocky ego in a "free" translation. What good's a poet without ego? Misplaced here, maybe.

Then what? Would you say it's just terminology? All we say is that if you want to fool around with what the man said, don't call it *translation?* Okay?

C.H.K.: *Good. Good. You know some bad translation's just laziness. Even people who know the language well. They guess at a word and destroy the sentence. Can't be bothered going back to the dictionary. Or the source. And you have to keep* asking.

V.MCH.: Yes. That's good.

C.H.K.: *Some people—old Legge, for example—had bad luck with their Chinese collaborators. Just not very good.*

V.MCH.: Not me, pal. I got lucky. Also, I suppose, there's the matter of time. If you're translating a French novel and the publisher's giving you a maximum $800 — But we don't need to get so fat about this. Me, anyhow. *I* should talk. What about that "War Year" poem we did?

C.H.K.: *Ohhh? The Ts'ao Sung? Did I tell you somebody wanted to reprint that on an antiwar calendar? But remember, we thought the original was pretty flat. Just another Confucian diatribe against war.*

V.MCH.: Yes, but we—or I, rather—got pretty far off it. Why did we want to do it anyhow? Because it had that strong ending about the corpses?

C.H.K.: *Yes. Yes. Do you have it?*

V.MCH.: Your literal version? Yes. It's here.

Marshland; / rivers(&)mountains / (have been)included / war map
Lowland;   territories   (into)

People; / (in)what / way; / (could)enjoy; / sticks(&)weeds
Population;   plan;   relish;

(I) request; / you / never / discuss / (military)promotion / matters
    ask;

One / general; / (after)achievements / made / 10,000; / bones; /
                                  numerous; corpses;
                                  (have) dried up;
                                    rotten

C.H.K.: *Yes. And you remember when we sent it out round-robin with the other poems to the consultants —*
V.MCH.: You sent it. That was *your* good idea. And how wonderfully kind they were, to bother with us!
C.H.K.: *— sent the first finished version, I mean, Dr. San-su Lin and her husband, Dr. Paul Lin, wrote us that the second line simply meant: "What can the (suffering) people do for a living now?" And here's our final version:*

    Lowland hills and rivers
                 dragged on to the war map
           O lowland lowlands O!
    Those groaning people!
              how can they live?
                 A turnip or two
                 grubbed up
    Don't talk to me
                about titles
                  promotions
                  all that slop
    One general
               pulling out a victory
         leaves
            ten
            thousand
            corpses
              to rot!

I like it. It's really better than the Mandarin.
V.MCH.: Oh, it's a *poem* all right, in English. But that quote from an English ballad! And the way I kept playing that

open O all through the first four lines. Well, we *did* want something outraged and sonorous. The taste's all right. But it's the furthest off an original we ever got.

You know I feel now that almost any getting away from the text—anything you're not forced into, I mean—is probably a mistake. I wonder at myself. Why didn't I try harder to do something with that "sticks and grass" in line two? It's better than the turnip thing. And closer. To the fact, I mean. Everything happens in Chinese famines. Clay-eating. Cannibalism.

But variation or not, you've got to have a good text to start with. And that's what you give me, my lad.

C.H.K.: *Hmm. But remember, that poem's an exception. Big exception. A few paraphrases like that in other poems. The rest are all very close. You know Achilles Fang and C.Y. Lee both said that.*

AXIOM : THE WORDS ARE, NOT THE POEM, AND THAT AIN'T ALL

A very good book of, and about, translation, *The Poem Itself,* edited by Stanley Burnshaw. But he makes a point we don't agree with: "The instant he [the translator] departs from the words of the original he departs from *its* poetry. For the words are the poem. . . ."

No. With qualifications. In the first place, if it were so—that's all, brother. No translation. Moreover—and Burnshaw isn't the first to put it—this argument seems to be where a lot of false notions about poetry and its translation come from.

There's a certain spastic rigidity in the doctrine. It seems to say, in part, that if you don't hang tight to the words, every translator can kick up his heels and gallop off on a horse of his own devising. True. He can. Why not? Let him. As we've seen, that's not translation in our book. But he may get a good poem out of it.

We still say no to the words-are-the-poem notion and

point out the simplest of reasons. It's possible—every schoolboy's done it—to translate a poem word for word with the most desperate fidelity and *not only not get* that *poem but get no poem at all.*

No. We say this: the words are the invariable original formula for the poem; what makes the reaction happen; the precise verbal incantation that evokes the event. Without the words, nothing. No poem. But just as the poet often, if not usually, intuits the poem long before he gets the precise words—otherwise, what's the point of revising and rewriting?—so the translator intuits the poem from its original formula and sets out to find a co-ordinate formula in English.

But once he gets off the tightrope of original words, how does he know where he'll land? Answer: wherever his sense of the poem coincides with the words, he sticks with them. If it doesn't, he questions the words over and over in order to dig out anything he may have missed. He may also look for help from the exegetes, who have built whole mountains of commentary in the Chinese.

There are times, however, when he must make a choice between word-stick and poem-stick. In that case he goes for the poem. But how can he be sure he's *got* the poem, or even that it's the one and only? He can't, of course. Poetry is not an area of rational certainties. But the jury of his peers will do.

C.H.K.: *Listen to this. It's from George Steiner's introduction to* The Penguin Book of Modern Verse Translation: *"That it is untranslatable is one of the definitions offered of poetry. . . ."*
V.MCH.: Okay. Let's pack up and go home.
C.H.K.: *"What remains after the attempt, intact and uncommunicated, is the original poem. So affirmed du Bellay, the French poet and rhetorician of the early sixteenth century, so, more recently, Robert Frost. . . ."*

V.MCH.: Yes, I saw that. It's all hoorah. Du Bellay didn't say any such damn thing. Not that *I've* been able to find in the *Défense et Illustration*. He *did* give bad translators hell. But he also speaks of "the laudable toil of translating." That poetry-is-untranslatable is just the final heresy of the words-are-the-poem school.

C.H.K.: *You must have a lot of faith in me.* [Laughs.] *I mean, not knowing Chinese.*

V.MCH.: Perfect trust. Hardly a character do I know. And what I know about the structure I got from you. Or from Fang and Liu. Or from Karlgren, especially *Sound and Symbol in Chinese.* What a beautiful piece of exposition!

C.H.K.: *Yes. Yes. Wonderful.*

V.MCH.: As wonderful, in its quite different way, as H. A. Calahan's *Learning to Sail.* And many a time when I was young I risked my neck on *that* one.

But what a glorious language, that Mandarin—and by T'ang times it was stripped down to an efficiency like a mathematical equation. The Mandarin at its most concise, and English now perhaps at its most multifarious. Marvelous confrontation!

But you know the great thing in translating Mandarin, the spooky and wonderful thing for me, is to see the unmistakable body of the poem begin to produce itself out of the barebones five or six or seven characters of the first line. Enough to make you believe there may be Jungian archetypes for poetry too. Why not?

And what's spookiest of all, to see that this is possible because the word order in Mandarin, lacking nearly all such pointers as articles, prepositions, inflections, or differentiation between the form of singular or plural, noun or verb or adjective, is nevertheless *precisely what we should regard as logical in English.* As against the word order in Latin, for example. It *makes sense* as English and as poem.

C.H.K.: *So we made the next jump in logic.*

V.MCH.: Exactly. Yes. You mean why not approximate that logic as faithfully as possible in English?

AXIOM : TO STICK AS CLOSE AS MAY BE TO THE INTENSE
MATHEMATICAL CONCISION OF THE CHINESE
AND CREATE STRUCTURES TO PROJECT THIS IN ENGLISH

Example:

1
(You)ask / me / why / (I)live(on) / emerald / mountain
               (for)what reason   green-jade   hill
                                     jade-green
                                     emerald-green

(I)smile / not / answer / (my)heart / natural(ly) / at ease
                                             at peace

peach / blossom(s) / (on)flow(ing) / water / quiet(ly) / far / go away
                                    stream

there is another / earth(&)sky / unlike / human world(below)
this is another   world

2
You asked what my reason is for lodging in the grey hills;
I smiled but made no reply, for my thoughts were idling on their own;
Like the flowers of the peach-tree borne by the stream, they had
    sauntered far away
To other climes, to other lands that are not in the World of Men.

3
You ask me:
               Why do I live
on this green mountain?
    I smile
    No answer
                  My heart serene
On flowing water
               peachblow
               quietly going
               far away

This is another earth
          another sky
No likeness
          to that human world below

4
Why do I live among the green mountains?
I laugh and answer not, my soul is serene:
It dwells in another heaven and earth belonging to no man.
The peach trees are in flower, and the water flows on. . . .

No. 1 is C.H.K.'s word-for-word rendering of Li Po's
"On the Mountain: Question and Answer." Arthur Waley
remarks that it's "particularly hard to translate satisfactor-
ily." No. 2 is his version. Our translation appears as No. 3,
and No. 4 comes from Shigeyoshi Obata's *The Works of Li
Po*.

The "grey" in Waley's second line is defensible enough.
For the character *ch'ing* Mathews gives: "The color of na-
ture; green, blue, black. A drab neutral tint." But we can't
help feeling that Waley works too hard to make an ingeni-
ous paraphrase of Li's bold plainness, even to the point of
what Robert Payne calls a "Miltonic overflow" (i.e., en-
jambment) in the third line. And that "sauntered"! Was he
trying for something a little John Clare-ish? Something
quietly iambic with an occasional tribrach or anapest?

Obata's version has an effect of delicate and averted sen-
sibility quite recognizably Japanese, as Waley's is English.
Our working, No. 3, tries to stay with Li's bold plainness
all the way, and with hardly an extra syllable in English.
The arrangement on the page promotes this, defines the
elements almost without punctuation, and knits the whole
thing together with such internal, head, or end rhymes as
green/serene and *no/flowing/peachblow/going/no/below*.

> AXIOM : THE POEM IS WHAT'S LEFT WHEN
> EVERYTHING ELSE HAS BEEN TRIED

As long ago as 1956 or '57 we got together one night at City Lights Bookstore in San Francisco with the hard-nosed intention of attacking a large body of classical Chinese poetry from the Han, say, into the Ch'ing. We wanted to put out the best damn translations anybody had yet brought into English.

A big order. Waley had a superb knowledge of Mandarin, but the ear of a second-string English Romantic. Glorious old Ezra—in *Cathay*, at least—was battling with the double opacity of two languages he didn't know, plus a suspect theory about the Chinese ideogram, plus the fact that everything had a tendency to turn out Pound rather than "Rihaku." Which isn't bad, either.

V.MCH.: Remember how he sent us greetings the night of the first "Poets' Follies" in San Francisco? And they turned out to be one of the *Cantos* somebody—was it Karlgren? No—had put into Swedish?

C.H.K.: *Yes, and you read it off from the stage without knowing a word of Swedish?*

VMCH.: Ha! That was the night I played King Thoas to the wickerwork Aphrodite from Saks Fifth Avenue. Been all over San Francisco looking for an actress to play Aphrodite. Nobody would go for it—but I had fun looking.

So I conned the design man at Saks into letting me borrow a wicker mannequin. Christian Dior was making them then.

"What's Aphrodite's sign?" he said.

"Oh," I said. "Fish. Scallop. Myrtle. Crescent moon."

He got out some gold cardboard and made her a necklace. Fish, scallop shells, lopsided stars. Gold crescent for the hair. Stunning. I carried her out to a cab under my arm and the doorman saluted.

We had a plan. Publish the translations first as a series of pamphlets, thirty or so to a pamphlet, at 25-35¢ each. A lot of people who were hooked on poetry couldn't afford it. We'd be the Haldeman-Juliuses of Chinese poetry. Then collect them in hardcover, and after that in paperback.

We found our man in another of the City Lights crowd, Harold Graves. He was just setting up his Golden Mountain Press—a rented IBM typewriter and a small used offset press—in an alley basement off Columbus Avenue. None of us had any money, so it must have been Shigeyoshi Murao, as usual, the manager at City Lights, who paid for paper, ink, and offset plates.

You went down some crumbly basement steps clogged with newspapers blown in from the street and let yourself in with your own key. (V. McH. had been appointed house editor and C.H.K. consultant.) Picked your way through a maze of stored furniture to the bright light and the sound of a running press at the rear. It was warm in there out of the blowy autumn night, and Harold, a sharp-talking ex-crew chief from the Eighth Air Force, would be working away with a can of tropical fruit juice at his elbow.

So we set to work collating sheets for the first pamphlet, *Why I Live on the Mountain.* C.H.K. had got his friend John Way, an excellent calligrapher, to do what amounted to a historical series of mutations in the character *hua*, meaning *quintessence*. We used one of these for the cover, plus letterpress in a French advertising script. Lawrence Ferlinghetti's City Lights Books did the distributing. This pamphlet and a second one, *The Lady and the Hermit*, between them sold eight or nine thousand copies before Harold's creditors closed in. Then we were out of business with a bang.

And if the whole thing reminds you of a miniscule *Illusions Perdues* without illusions—well, it *was* a little like that. Fun.

AXIOM : MORE THAN DRONE OR DRIP OR IAMB,
THE SIMPLE DECLARATIVE VERB IS THE CURSE
OF ENGLISH POETRY AND TRANSLATION

Or almost any verb you can avoid, for that matter. What you were told in rhetoric classes is all wrong. Most verbs don't add zing to a sentence. They *describe* action. They don't *make* it. Functionally, they're discourse, not poetry. (With the usual exceptions.) Many an oral sentence—and why not in poetry?—works better with nothing but a participle. Or no verb at all.

Or haven't you noticed?

About the time the first plates on *Mountain* were getting dim and we were beginning to think about a revised edition, C.H.K. brought a friend around one night and introduced us. For a while after that he was almost a third collaborator.

He was just in from Hong Kong and he had one of those traditional Chinese first names. Call him Yao. A Fukien man from southeast China, but his looks and style—utterly without affectation, by the way—were those of an international French intellectual *à la* Malraux. Much younger, of course. He was also—again, utterly without affectation or indeed serious effort on his part—purely *simpatico* to women, though he seemed to get into very complicated relations with them, relations involving some extremely high-minded notions of what was honorable between the sexes. I suppose they loved it. He had a letter from the American consul in Hong Kong, the most powerful recommendation we'd ever seen from an American official.

Yao had been a colonel of infantry in Chiang's army during World War II. When the Communists took over, he went back in as one of Chiang's agents—though he had no high regard for Chiang—and got out again to Hong Kong with certain hot breaths on his neck. Then in he went again, this time as an American agent, and returned once more a step ahead of the hand reaching for his shoulder. But the third time, when he was asked to go in as an agent for both Chiang and the Americans—and spy on each for the other?—he refused, though the salary was extravagant. China was his country, he said.

We didn't pretend to understand this completely. He didn't, in fact, talk about it. V.McH. got it second-hand from C.H.K. In any case, Yao's wife, a European dancer, denounced him for idiocy and left him. He took it hard. For a while, with a partner who was an ex-Nationalist general, he made a living as a singer in a Hong Kong nightclub. Then he got a job as chief interpreter at the American consulate in Hong Kong. His work was screening applicants for American entry and in time he managed it for himself.

And what had he been singing in the nightclub? Some of the very poems we were translating. He was one of the few people left in the world who knew the music they'd been sung to, handed down by scholars from the T'ang and Sung. He'd learned the tunes from one of his teachers in Fukien Province.

Yao soon found a good spot for himself with the State Department. But he was in trouble for a while after he landed in San Francisco. Chinatown wasn't happy with the new breed of well-sifted intellectual immigrants and he couldn't get a job. He was living in a dingy yellow-brick Chinese boarding house on what had once been the old Barbary Coast. We used to bring him food. A paper sack of apples, or fried rice from Sam Wo's. We'd squeeze into the alley and call up at his lighted window until he came down to let us in.

C.H.K.: *Remember that place? He had his paintings all round the room.*

V.MCH.: Um. Weren't they strange? A combination of classical Chinese and late nineteenth-century Western academic. Pretty competent technically. And those superb color photographs of Hong Kong! I used to puzzle over him. How all this stuff went together—the music and poetry and the secret-agenting.

C.H.K.: *And you know he was a swimming champion in*

Hong Kong. Remember the cups? Inscribed. I was just thinking of the night we worked on that Li Po "Night Mooring at Cow's Creek." Revising it.

V.MCH.: You and Yao did. The Mandarin lost me early. I didn't get back in the game until you explained what you'd worked out and I had to find a formula for it. Here's the early version:

> At Cow's Creek
> > on Western River
> > > the night
>
> Sky still blue
> > not a rag of cloud
>
> I go on deck
> > to look at the bright moon
>
> thinking of
> > the great General Hsieh of old
>
> I myself
> > can chant a poem
>
> but that man
> > cannot hear me
>
> In the morning
> > we make sail and go
>
> The maple leaves
> > fall as they will

C.H.K.: *Yes. Yes. I remember. The trouble was in the first two lines of the second quatrain.*

V.MCH.: You two got it worked out finally and explained over and over what it *could* mean. I kept trying this and that, and when I got it

> I also
> > can make poetry
>
> but that man's like
> > will not be found again

we all yelled and shouted.

C.H.K.: *Yes. Five-syllable lines. You know I didn't realize until about fifteen years ago that the* older *Chinese poetry* always *had an even number of syllables in the standard line. It wasn't until later, mainly in the T'ang, that the influence of foreign music, foreign tunes, brought in uneven lines. One syllable to a line, three, five, nine, eleven— anything to fit the tune. That was the t'zu.*

V.MCH.: That's what Yao sings mainly?

C.H.K.: *Yes. So the way we break it up on the page is really in accord with that. That convention. I always have the feeling any verse that runs vertically has a timeless value whereas horizontal lines are limited in time. By time?*

V.MCH.: Hey! That's good.

C.H.K.: *Remember I told you Professor Chen Shih-hsiang at Berkeley said something like that when he saw the first pamphlet? He's an excellent Chinese poet himself. He said it had "an architectural beauty that no other translations of Chinese poetry ever did have."*

And one night we drove Yao up to Lawrence Ferlinghetti's wonderful old reclaimed Italianate Victorian house on Potrero Hill to put a score or so of the translations on tape. V.McH. was to read each poem in English and Yao would sing it in Mandarin to the old tune. We fussed and fumed for a while beside the snapping piñon fire. V.McH. thought his voice was too heavy for the lines and Yao wasn't sure he had the tune straight. They settled down finally, and everyone in the room was charmed with the nostalgic clarity of Yao's baritone in that all-but-forgotten music.

AXIOM : THE TRANSLATOR OF POETRY SHOULD TAKE
THE TROUBLE TO BE BORN A GREAT POET

Which will do until we learn a little more—and also until we discover where we have been wrong.

Design by David Bullen
Typeset in Mergenthaler Sabon
by Robert Sibley
Printed by Maple-Vail
on acid-free paper